Full fathom five thy father lies;

Of his bones of coral made:

Those are pearls that were in his eyes;

Nothing of him that doth fade,

But doth suffer a sea-change

Into something rich and strange.

William Shakespeare
(The Tempest)

Ian Macdonald Smith

Bermuda Triangles

Thanks go to my friends and family, without whose help I would certainly fare worse. Great thanks go to Niall Woolf, whose friendship, support and talent have been humbling, and to David Cox, who continues to amuse and be there, both to whom I will always be grateful.

As with the production of any book, many people have contributed to its completion. Their efforts, when combined, have made a big difference - thank you all.

A few in particular have had more impact: Niall helped edit and place slides with quotes; Philip Ridge designed the basic layout for this project; Peter Matchum created the map; Gerry Brashier helped crystallize my words and Steve Roper organized the printing.

Other titles:
"A Scape to Bermuda".
Limited edition prints and books available.

Copyright © 1993
Ian Macdonald-Smith
17 Jennings Road, Smith's, Bermuda.

ISBN 976-8104-66-X

Printed and bound in Hong Kong by Book Art Inc., Toronto

The number of rational hypotheses that can explain any given phenomenon is infinite.
Phaedrus

Mention the Bermuda Triangle to practically anyone and they will tell you it is the area where ships, planes and people mysteriously disappear without trace or logical explanation, yet few can actually tell you where Bermuda is. The Island is but one point on the infamous Triangle but because it shares equal billing in the name, it has received all the notoriety while the other shores and islands that the same triangle touches go largely unnoticed and unmentioned.

Ever since the new world was discovered, Bermuda has been the subject of one tall tale after another, to an extent hardly warranted by the size of this tiny archipelago. Bermuda was initially dubbed the "Isles of Devils" after its discovery in 1503 because of the wailing noises that superstitious sailors heard as they passed close to the Island en route between Europe and the New World. There's no denying that this remote Island was very unforgiving to vessels which strayed too close to its treacherous reefs, so it was fear of the unknown which gave Bermuda its dubious reputation in the 16th and 17th centuries. The devilish sounds that so frightened the mariners of old, turned out to be nothing more than the wind in the trees, the pounding surf and the cries of the Cahow, an incredibly docile bird to its later detriment. The famous Elizabethan bard did little to help when it was rumoured his play "The Tempest" was inspired by Bermuda! Thus the island was romanticized, vilified and mythicized from the beginning.

Bermuda, a 20 square mile rock, and the only obstacle in thousands of square miles of open ocean, should have been easy to miss. However, there are more old wrecks snared on the Island's 254 square miles of reefs than there are disappearances attributed to the whole of the Bermuda Triangle! After the landmark shipwreck of 1609 and the advent of permanent settlers in 1612, most of the myths about Bermuda were quickly dispelled and the Island slowly gained the reputation of a paradise on earth. It is strange that almost four centuries later the Island remains in the public eye with a recurrence of its former reputation for danger due in the main to excessive commercialization of the Triangle myth, fueled by extended media hype, and a plethora of books and documentaries about the Triangle from the well researched and scientific to those based mostly on hearsay and rumour - and still going. While there is no argument that there have been some strange incidents in the area, maybe moreso than other areas of the world, there are also rational explanations for these occurrences and while they may not completely dispel the myth, they are certainly enlightening.

The "Legend" of the Bermuda Triangle was brought to the public's attention in 1950, in what was possibly one of the duller moments of media history, by a journalist called E.V.W. Jones. His exposé has been a media favourite hashed over for the past 40 years and it is not hard to understand why. What a story! Numerous boats and a few planes disappear in a given area with no proven explanation or wreckage. Other journalists, no doubt anxious to cash in on the public's sudden interest in the Triangle, enthusiastically reported other strange disappearances of vessels which were later found to be nowhere near the the Triangle's designated area.

It was not until 1975 that the extent of the artistic licence taken was revealed by Lawrence David Kusche in his book "The Bermuda Triangle Mystery - Solved". In this book Mr. Kusche analyzed each disappearance and revealed either horrendous weather in the area at that time, or proof that the vessel in question was not fit for the high seas. While this was a well researched book and worth reading, it still left questions about the Bermuda Triangle unanswered.

Mother Nature also plays a significant part in the mystery, for where the warm Gulf Stream waters and the cold Northern currents meet in the Western Atlantic, the seas are turbulent and unpredictable. At times the ocean is like a mirror, then so quickly will a major storm form that the world's most advanced technology will not detect it in sufficient time to provide adequate warning.

Bermudians daily observe the awesome power and majesty of nature from their isolated, reef-protected oasis and in stormy weather wonder how any vessel could survive the ocèan's wrath. From this panoramic spot, residents have no problem believing that natural phenomena are the logical explanation for many of the Triangle's disappearances. Beyond media hype and tall tales, however, there have been some intriguing theories advanced to help explain the disappearances of ships and planes in the area. For those interested I'd like to include one.

The Hydrate Theory, first proposed by Dr. Richard MacIver, partially explains some disappearances merely by the Laws of Probability. Hydrates were discovered in the laboratory in 1810 but it was not until 1964 that natural hydrates were found. Methane hydrate is a frozen gas that is formed only in the presence of water and under very specific temperatures and high atmospheric pressures. The gas is created by decomposing matter on the oceanbed and exists in substantial layers on top of the rockbed of the Continental Shelf, off the Eastern United States. On occasion the shelf succumbs to erosion and tremors, triggering massive underwater slides. These slides cause the methane hydrate to be released and from the abyssal depths a mass of methane bubbles rises, ever expanding, to the surface. Very little, if anything, can float on this gas.

The result of these underwater slides is that they leave massive volumes of gas on the surface of the water which later rise high into the atmosphere. There have been many sightings of fog and mists away from coastal waters that can be explained by these methane clouds. Methane's existence on the Earth's surface explains some of the other mysterious circumstances encountered in the Bermuda Triangle.

There have been many stories of engine and electronic failure in the air and on the ocean. When any motorized vehicle passes through a cloud of methane gas, the engine is starved of the oxygen necessary to power it. Ships have been found completely devoid of life or with only skeletal remains on board. The crew's demise could certainly have been the result of asphyxiation from methane inhalation.

When released methane rises to the surface, the water becomes agitated, producing negative ionization. This ionization creates magnetic fields that are responsible for other common factors experienced within the Bermuda Triangle - compasses spinning and preventing accurate readings being taken and electronic failure. Rising methane gas could presumably cause similar things to happen to airplane compasses and electronics. Certainly, if this is the case, the F19 squadron which disappeared in December 1945, was flying low enough to be affected.

In addition to the disappearances, there have been sightings of UFOs and strange lights in the area. Such sightings are certainly not exclusive to the Bermuda Triangle and while there is no explanation for them yet, this should not detract from the progress made to rationalize the Bermuda Triangle. People tend to create myths when they don't have the answers to problems and this certainly leads to further confusion. It is subsequently much harder to arrive at the truth, as the truth is often less appealing than the myth. Those whose insatiable curiosity leads them in a quest for the solution to the myth of the Bermuda Triangle would be wise to support the research of those institutions most capable of providing the scientific world with credible truths.

Bermuda Triangles makes no attempt to solve the mystery. Rather it explores the endless wealth of triangles found on the Island, in its buildings and natural beauty. The photographs and quotations symbolically conform to the six cycles of life according to Pythagoras: Birth (4-15), Growth and Decay (16-150), Death (151-168), Absorption (169-192) and Metamorphosis (193-208).

Bermuda Triangles provides an alternative way of viewing aspects of architecture and nature which can be broken down geometrically. Please enjoy what happens to your perception when you treat each image as a mathematical puzzle. By seeing how many triangles reside in each image you may see the whole from a new perspective.

I have always believed and still believe that artists who live and work with spiritual values cannot and should not remain indifferent to a conflict in which the highest values of humanity and civilization are at stake.
Pablo Picasso

Man is preceded by forest, followed by desert.

Graffiti

The larger the island of knowledge,

the longer the shoreline of wonder.

Ralph W. Sockman

The Way is like an empty vessel

that yet may be drawn from.

Lao-Tzu

The pyramids themselves, doting with age,

have forgotten the names of their founders.

Thomas Fuller

Life's troubled bubble broken.

Walter De La Mare

I wonder if we could contrive…some magnificent myth that would in itself carry conviction to our whole community.

Plato

*Science must begin with myths, and
with the criticism of myths.*

Sir Karl Popper

*The process of scientific discovery is, in effect,
a continual flight from wonder.*

Albert Einstein

*The beginning of wisdom is
the definition of terms.*

Socrates

Here is the beginning of philosophy; a recognition of the conflicts between men, a search for their cause, a condemnation of mere opinion...and the discovery of a standard of judgment.

Epictetus

'What's new?' is an interesting and broadening question, but one in which, if pursued exclusively, results only in an endless parade of trivia and fashion, the silt of tomorrow. I would like, instead, to be concerned with the question 'What is best?', a question which cuts deeply rather than broadly, a question whose answers tend to move the silt downstream.

Robert M. Pirsig

Miracles are so called because they excite wonder. In unphilosophical minds any rare or unexpected thing excites wonder, while in philosophical minds the familiar excites wonder also.

George Santayana

The truth knocks on the door and you say,
'Go away, I'm looking for the truth,'
and so it goes away. Puzzling.

Robert M. Pirsig

Why shouldn't truth be stranger than fiction?

Fiction, after all, has to make sense.

Mark Twain

There is only one truth, and 'this too must change'.

Chinese Proverb

Truth is rarely pure, and never simple.

Oscar Wilde

Our civilization...has not yet fully recovered from the shock of its birth - the transition from the tribal society or 'closed society', with its submission to magical forces, to the 'open society' which sets free the critical powers of man.

Sir Karl Popper

I do not feel obliged to believe that the same God who has endowed us with sense, reason and intellect has intended us to forego their use.

Galileo Galilei

Philosophy removes from religion all reason for existing. As the science of the spirit, it looks upon religion as a phenomenon, a transitory historical fact, a psychic condition that can be surpassed.

Benedetto Croce

There is a good saying that if triangles invented a god, they would make him three-sided.

Charles, Baron De Montesquieu

The fundamental fact about the Greek was that he had top use of his mind. The ancient priests had said, 'Thus far and no further. We set the limits of thought.' The Greeks said, 'All things are to be examined and called into question. There are no limits set on thought.'

Edith Hamilton

To become a popular religion, it is only necessary for a superstition to enslave a philosophy.

W. R. Inge

It is conceivable that religion may be morally useful
without being intellectually sustainable.

John Stuart Mill

There is only one religion though there
are a hundred versions of it.

George Bernard Shaw

A faith that cannot survive collision with the

truth is not worth many regrets.

Arthur C. Clarke

Don't wait for the Last Judgement.

It takes place every day.

Albert Camus

I respect faith but doubt is what

gets you an education.

Wilson Mizner

The salvation of mankind lies only in making

everything the concern of all.

Alexander Solzhenitsyn

*Education is simply the soul of a society as it passes
from one generation to another.*

G. K. Chesterton

Education is the transmission of civilization.

Will and Ariel Durant

Teaching is not a lost art, but the regard for it is a lost tradition.

Jaques Barzun

To teach is to learn.

Japanese Proverb

Learn to reason forward and backward on both sides of the question.

Thomas Blandi

Let us train our minds to desire

what the situation demands.

Seneca

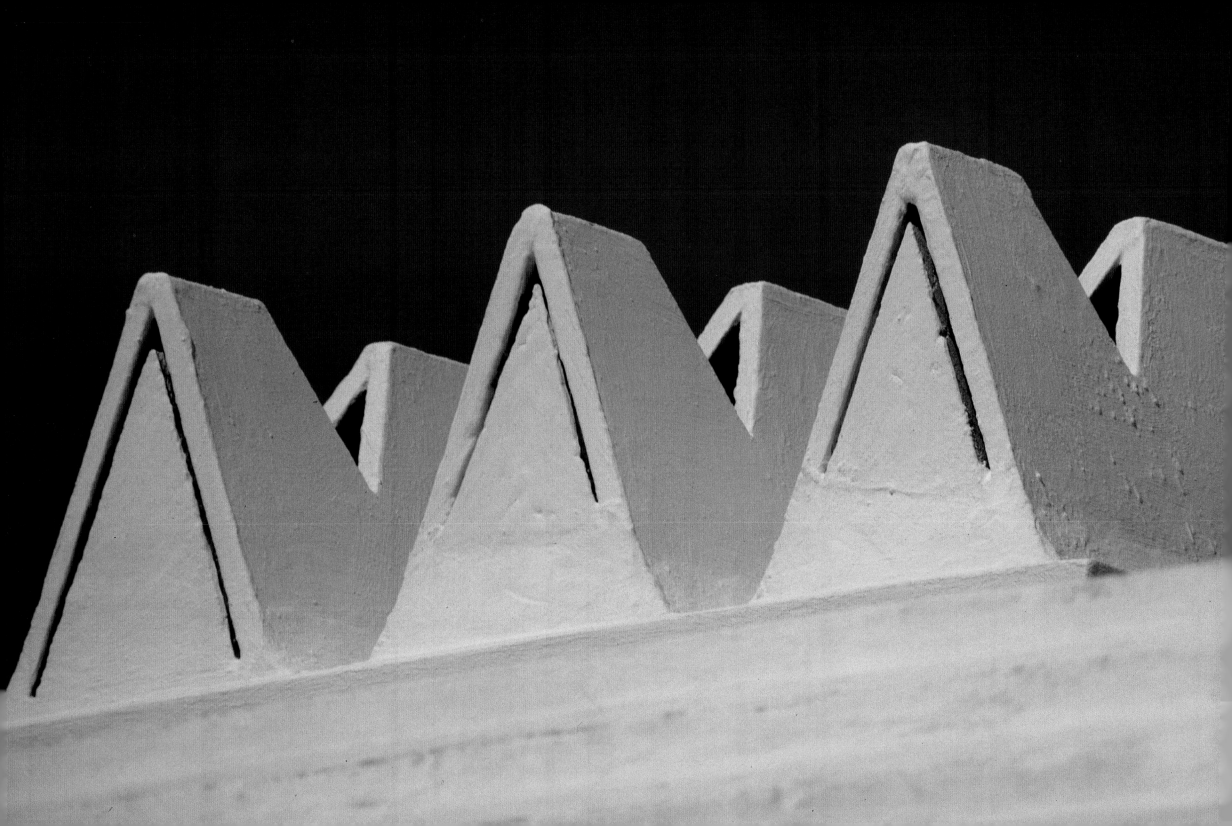

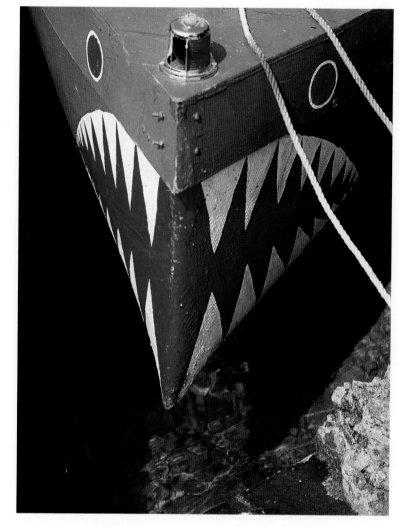

A powerful idea communicates some of its strength

to him who challenges it.

Marcel Proust

There is one thing stronger than all the armies in the world:

and that is an idea whose time has come.

Victor Hugo

A book is the only place in which you can examine a
fragile thought without breaking it, or explore an
explosive idea without fear it will go off in your
face...It is one of the few havens remaining
where a [person's] mind can get both
provocation and privacy.

Edward P. Morgan

Those who decide to use leisure as a means of mental
development, who love good music, good books,
good pictures, good plays, good company,
good conversation - what are they?
They are the happiest people
in the world.

William Lyon Phelps

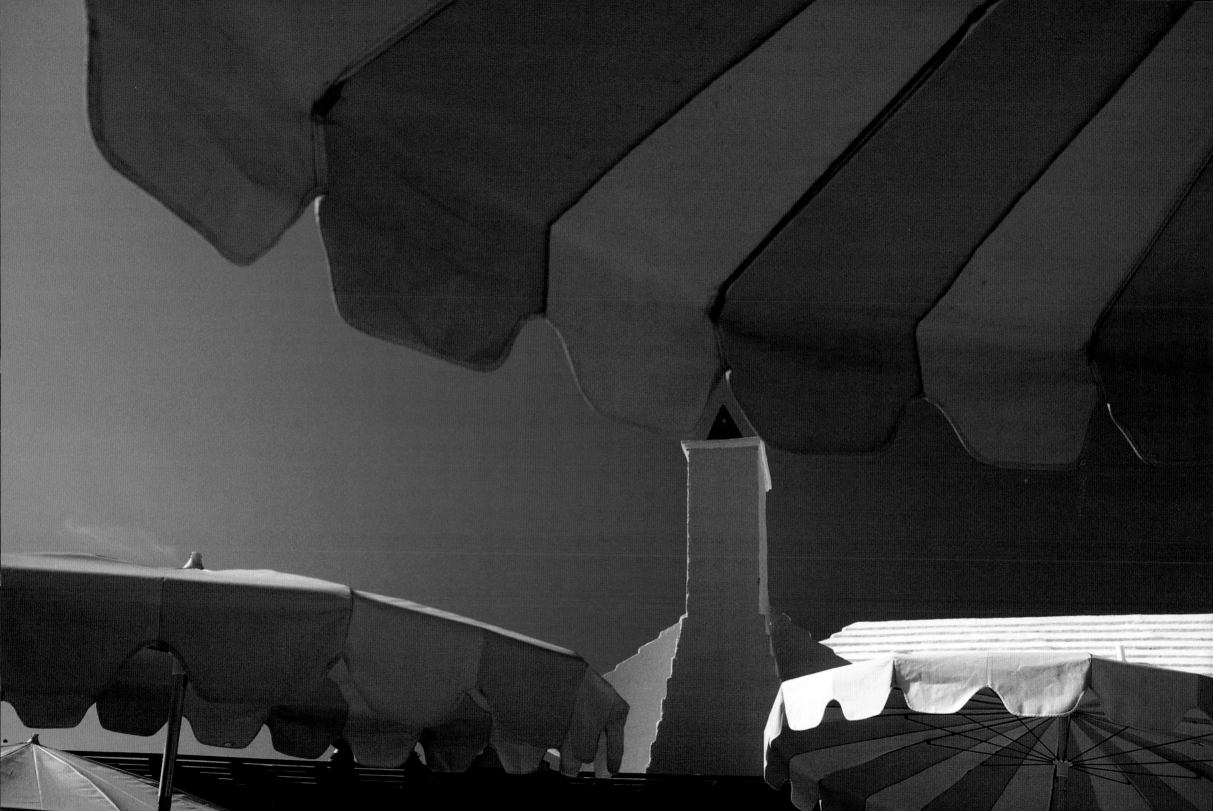

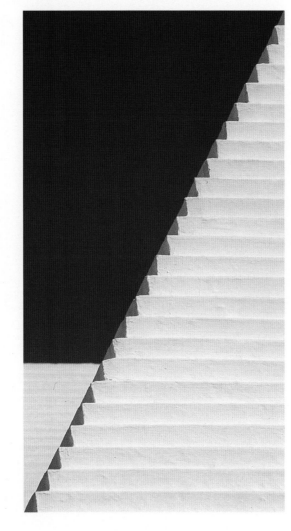

Happy is he who has been able to

learn the cause of things.

Virgil

Taste all, and hand the knowledge down.

Gary Snyder

The multitude of books is making us ignorant.

Voltaire

To know all things is not permitted.

Horace

Do not read, as children do, to amuse yourself, or like the ambitious,
for the purpose of instruction. No, read in order to live.

Gustave Flaubert

The things taught in schools and colleges are not an education,

but the means of education.

Ralph Waldo Emerson

The reason parents no longer lead their children in the right direction
is because the parents aren't going that way themselves.

Frank McKinney Hubbard

From the earliest of times the old have rubbed it into the young that they are
wiser than they, and before the young had discovered what nonsense this was
they were too old, and it profited them to carry in the imposture.

W. Somerset Maugham

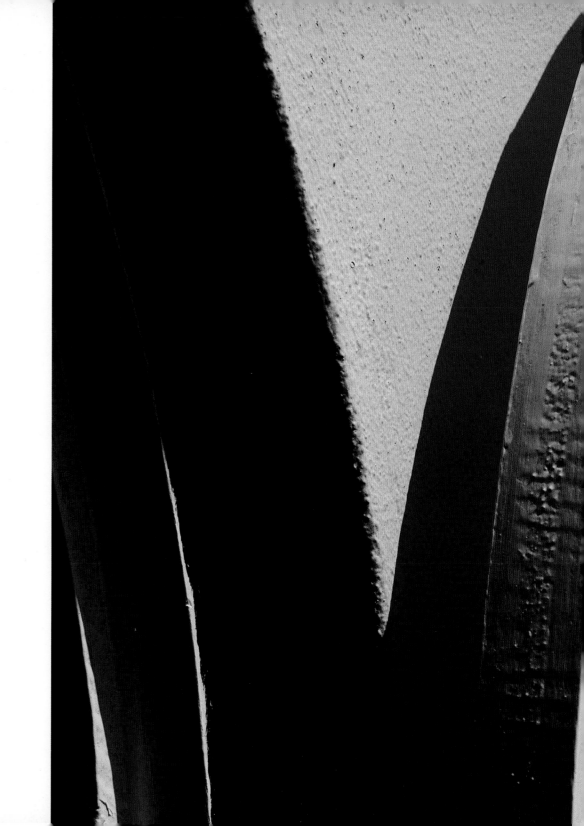

Any subject can be effectively taught in some intellectually honest form to any child at any stage of development.

Jerome Bruner

A child miseducated is a child lost.

John F. Kennedy

We need to make a world in which fewer children are born,

and in which we take better care of them.

Dr. George Wald

A society which practices death control must at the same time practice birth control.

John Rock

War will never cease until babies begin to come into the world with
larger cerebrums and smaller adrenal glands.

H. L. Mencken

All who have meditated on the art of mankind have been convinced

that the fate of empires depends on the education of youth.

Aristotle

I confess that any hopefulness for the future of civilization is based on a reasonable expectation that humanity is still only beginning its course.

W. R. Inge

Civilization is the encouragement of differences. Civilization thus becomes a synonym of democracy. Force, violence, pressure, or compulsion with a view to conformity, is both uncivilized and undemocratic.

Mohandas Gandhi

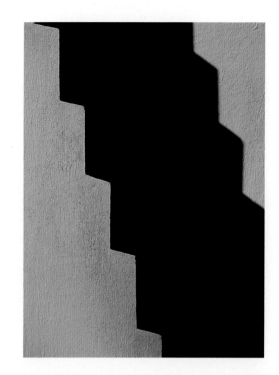

Leaders have a significant role in creating the state of mind that is society.

John Gardner

There will be no end to the troubles of states, or indeed... of humanity itself, till philosophers become kings in this world, or till those we now call kings and rulers really and truly become philosophers.

Plato

The politicians of our time might be characterized
by their vain attempts to change the world
and by their inability to change themselves.

George Faludy

The village had institutionalized all human functions in forms of
low intensity...Participation was high and organisation was low.
This is the formula for stability.

Marshall McLuhan

Power does not corrupt. Fear corrupts,

perhaps the fear of loss of power.

John Steinbeck

Power undirected by high purpose spells calamity; and high purpose by itself

is utterly useless if the power to put it into effect is lacking.

Theodore Roosevelt

The greater the power the more dangerous the abuse.

Edmund Burke

Under current law, it is a crime for a private citizen to lie to a government

official, but not for the government official to lie to the people.

Donald M. Frazer

Therein the problem...lies.

Graffiti

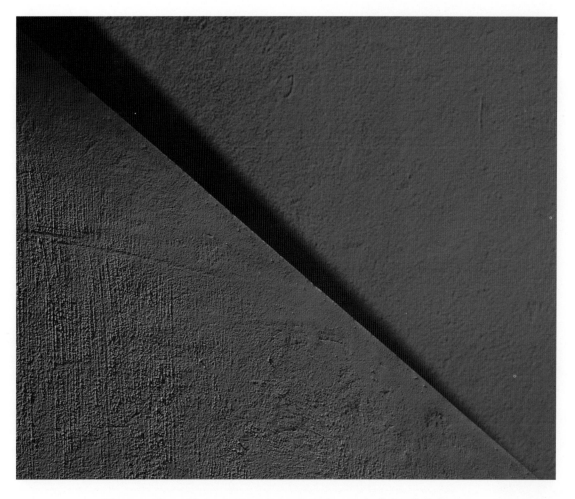

There are three sides to every story - yours, mine, and all that lie between.

Jody Kern

Where is there dignity unless there is honesty?

Tullius Cicero

I think that there is nothing, not even crime, more opposed to poetry, to philosophy, ay, to life itself than this incessant business.

Henry David Thoreau

Capitalism was doomed ethically before it was doomed economically, a long time ago.

Alexander Solzhenitsyn

One of the weaknesses of our age is our apparent inability
to distinguish our needs from our greeds.

Don Robinson

It is the preoccupation with possession, more than anything else, that prevents men from living freely and nobly.

Bertrand Russell

We live in a vastly complex society which has been able to provide us with a multitude of material things, and this is good, but people are beginning to suspect that we have paid a high spiritual price for our plenty.

Euell Gibbons

Our concern is not how to worship in the catacombs but

how to remain human in the skyscrapers.

Abraham Joshua Heschel

Clearly, then, the city is not a concrete jungle,

it is a human zoo.

Desmond Morris

The principle aspect of the electric age is that it establishes a global network that has much of

the character of our central nervous system.

Marshall McLuhan

We are citizens of the world; and the tragedy of our times is that we do not know this.

Woodrow Wilson

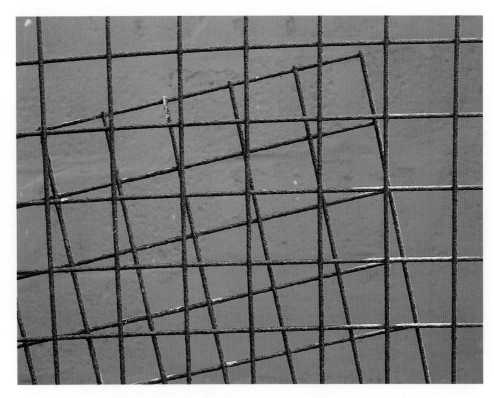

We are locked into a system of 'fouling our own nest' so long as we behave as

independent, rational free-enterprisers.

Garrett Hardin

The fouling of the nest which has been typical of man's activity in the past on a local scale now seems

to be extending to the whole system.

Kenneth Boulding

It becomes increasingly obvious to all countries that the uneven distribution and consumption of resources...is morally, ethically, and practically unacceptable.

Moshe Safdie

The essential cause of environmental pollution is over-population.

Jon Breslaw

The most alarming of all man's assaults upon the environment is the contamination of air, earth, rivers, and sea...this pollution is for the most part irrecoverable.

Rachel Carson

The most important pathological effects of pollution are extremely delayed and indirect.

Rene Dubos

Pollution is nothing but the resources we are not harvesting.
We allow them to disperse because we have been
ignorant of their value.

Buckminster Fuller

To look to private business for solutions to pollution may
be futile. Its horizons are deliberately limited to those
factors which are considered to be of immediate
importance, principally economic, and the
hidden costs to the society at large
tend to be ignored.

Frank M. Potter, Jr.

Are you not ashamed of heaping up the greatest amount of money and honour and reputation, and caring so little about wisdom and truth and the greatest improvement of the soul?

Socrates

Private enterprise, indeed, became too private.
It became privileged enterprise, not free enterprise.

Franklin Delano Roosevelt

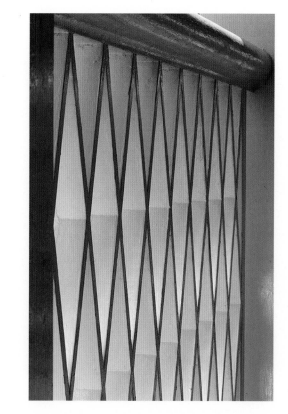

We must have a political state powerful enough to deal with corporate wealth, but how are we going to keep that state with its augmenting power from being captured by the force we want it to control?

Vernon Louis Parrington

It is probably safe to say that over a long period of time, political morality has been as high as business morality.

Henry Steele Commager

Do you imagine that a state can submit and not be overthrown, in which decisions of law have no power, but are set aside and trampled upon by individuals?

Socrates

Civilization is a race between

education and catastrophe.

H. G. Wells

The higher the individualism, the higher must be the socialism. The resultant of these opposing forces...must be determined by each age for itself.

Henry Demarest Lloyd

Democracy passes into despotism.

Plato

Treat all men alike. Give them all the same laws. Give them all an even chance to live and grow.

Chief Joseph

The best things and the best people rise out of their separateness; I'm

against a homogenized society because I want the cream to rise.

Robert Frost

The worst form of inequality is to try and make unequal things equal.

Aristotle

Equality of opportunity is an equal opportunity to prove unequal talents.

Sir Herbert Samuel

It is not easy for men to emerge from obscurity

if their qualities are thwarted by

narrow means at home.

Juvenal

Our inequality materializes our upper classes,

vulgarizes our middle class, brutalizes

our lower classes.

Matthew Arnold

Poverty is the mother of crime.

Marcus Aurelius

The forgotten man at the bottom of the economic pyramid.

Franklin Delano Roosevelt

Hope is a good breakfast,

but it is a bad supper.

Francis Bacon

Necessity knows no laws.

Pubilius Syrus

Never in this world can hatred be stilled by hatred; it will only be stilled by non-hatred.

This is the law Eternal.

Buddha

Must the hunger become anger and the anger fury before anything will be done?

John Steinbeck

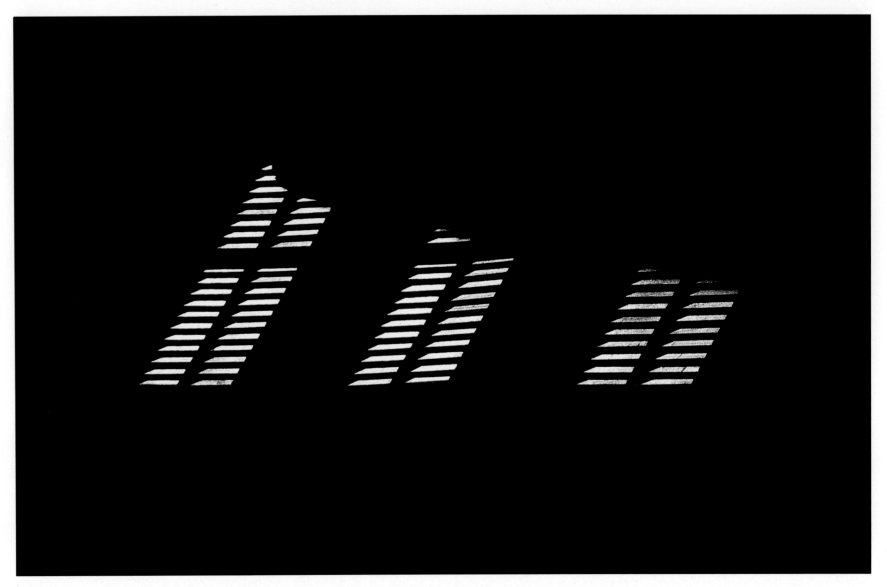

We shall have to repent in this generation, not so much for the evil deeds of the wicked people, but for the appalling silence of the good people.

Dr. Martin Luther King, Jr.

Prejudice is the reason of fools.

Voltaire

I have a little shadow that goes in and out with me,
And what can be the use of him is more than I can see.

Robert Louis Stevenson

An individual is as strong as his or her prejudice. Two things reduce
prejudice - education and laughter.

Dr. Laurence J. Peter

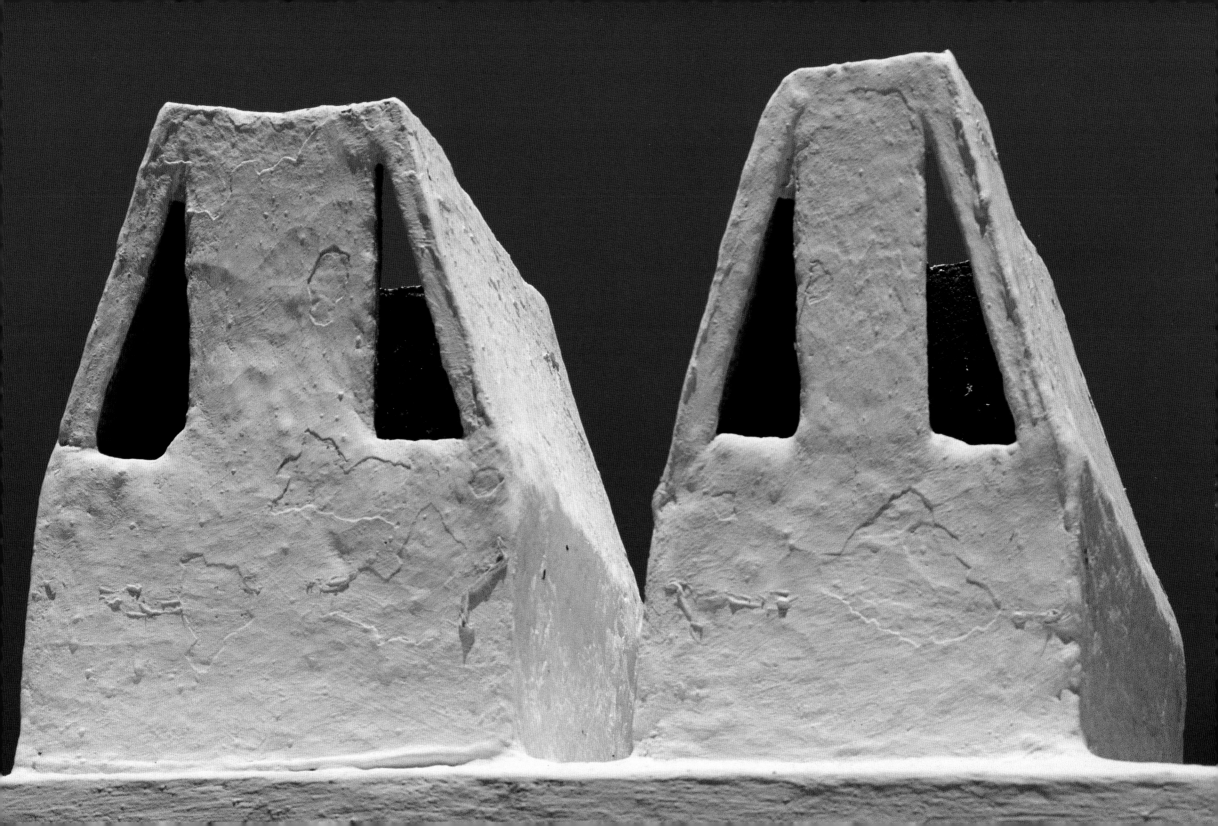

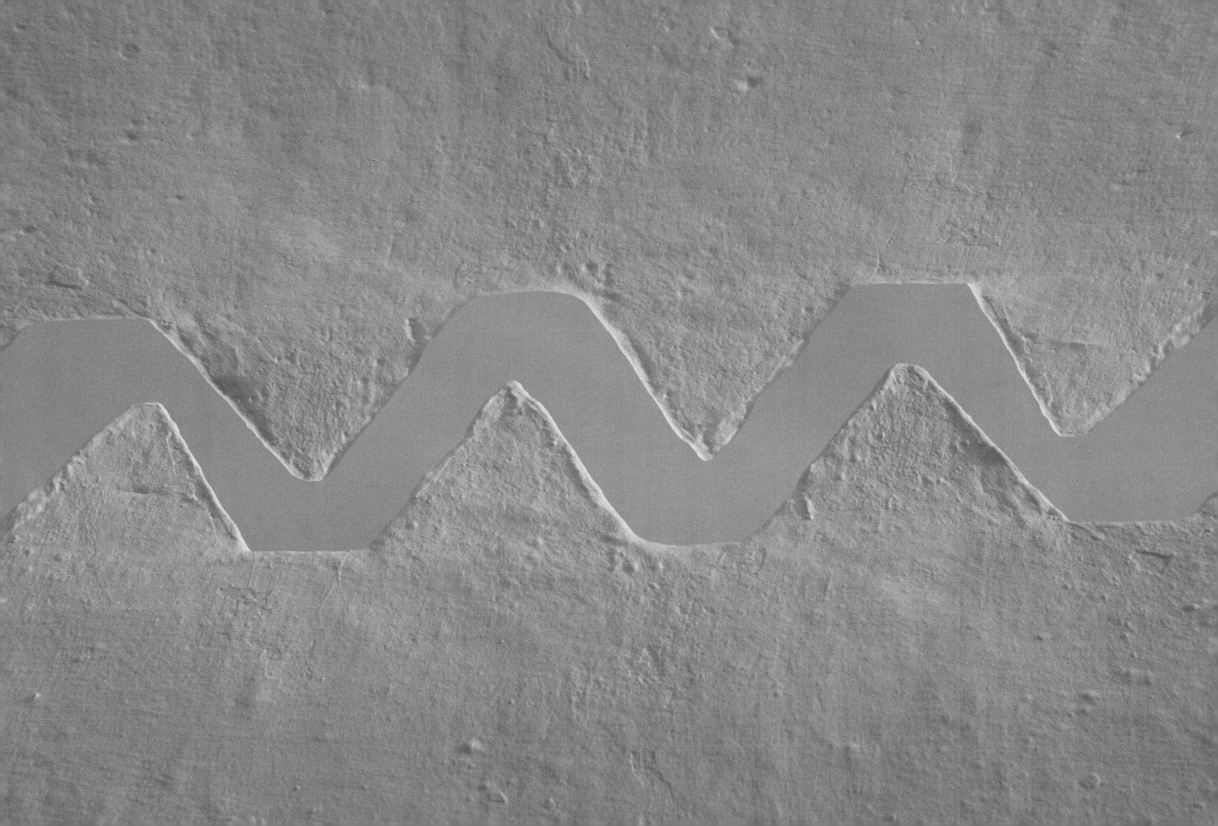

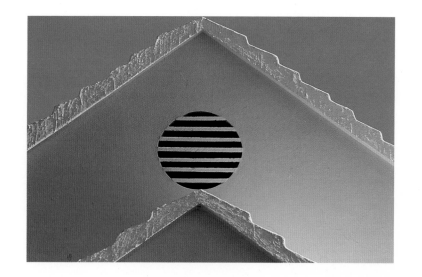

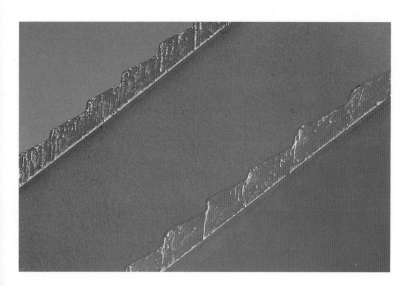

There are three things I always forget.
Names, faces and - the third I can't remember.

Italo Svevo

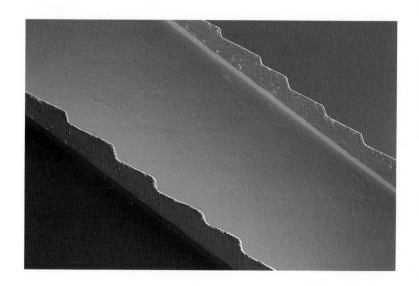

A little more of the abstract and we'd have gone potty. What is there to bite on in the abstract?
You may as well eat triangles and go to bed with a sewing machine.

Joyce Cary

If you don't know where you are going, you will probably end up somewhere else.

Laurence J. Peter

One day the don't knows will get in, and then where will we be?

Spike Milligan

Perfection of means and confusion of ends seems to characterize our age.

Albert Einstein

Any intelligent fool can make things bigger, more complex and more violent. It takes a touch of genius

- and a lot of courage - to move in the opposite direction.

E. F. Schumacher

We live in a Newtonian world of Einsteinian physics ruled by Frankenstein logic.

David Russell

As far as the laws of mathematics refer to reality, they are not certain,

and as far as they are certain, they do not refer to reality.

Albert Einstein

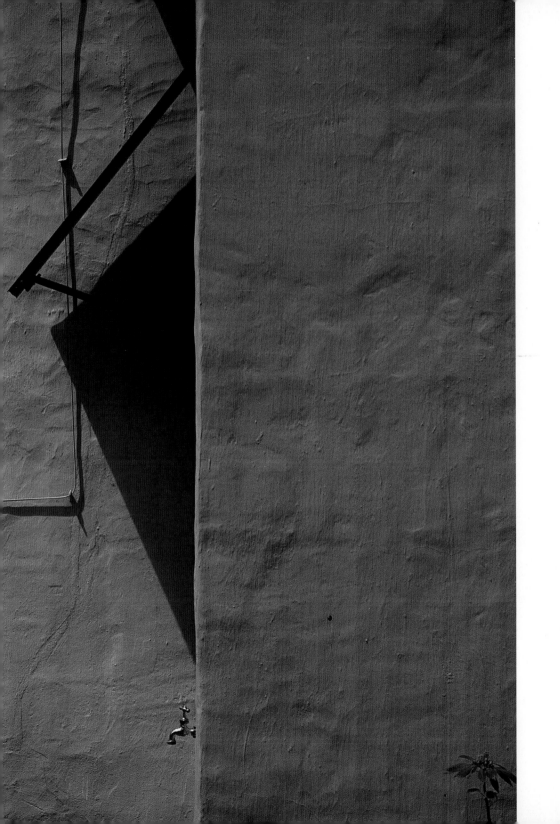

One geometry be more true than another;
it can only be convenient.
Geometry is not true, it is advantageous.

Robert M. Pirsig

Mathematics, rightly viewed, possesses not only truth, but supreme beauty
- a beauty cold and austere, like that of sculpture.

Bertrand Russell

The highest possible stage of moral culture is when we recognize that we ought to control our thoughts.

Charles Darwin

There's only one corner of the universe you can be certain of improving, and that's of your own self.

Aldous Huxley

Peace is an armistice in a war that is continuously going on.

Thucydides

A man is only ethical when life, as such, is sacred to him, that of plants and
animals as well as that of his fellow man, and when he devotes himself
helpfully to all life that is in need of help.

Albert Schweitzer

Who ought to be fonder of peace than those suffering

from nothing but war.

Niccolo Machiavelli

Man - a being in search of meaning.

Plato

...the thoughts of Plato and Machiavelli...don't seem quite enough armour for a world beset with splitting the atoms, urban guerrillas, nineteen varieties of psychotherapists, amplified guitars, napalm, computers, astronauts, and an atmosphere polluted simultaneously with auto exhaust and TV commercials.

John Fischer

Ever since our love for machines replaced the love we used to have for our fellow man, catastrophes proceed to increase.

Man Ray

Women have always been the guardians of wisdom and humanity which makes them natural, but usually secret, rulers. The time has come for them to rule openly, but together with and not against men.

Charlotte Woolf

Endure and preserve yourselves for better things.

Virgil

Change your thoughts and you change your world.

Norman Vincent Peale

Each man the architect of his own fate.

Appius Caecus

Our patience will achieve more than our force.

Edmund Burke

We keep passing unseen through little moments
of other people's lives.

Robert M. Pirsig

It is our noticing them that puts things in a room, our growing used to them that takes them away again and clears a space for us.

Marcel Proust

We are so made that we can enjoy intense enjoyment from a contrast and very little from a state of things.

Sigmund Freud

Everything should be made as simple as possible, but not simpler.

Albert Einstein

Less is more.

Mies van der Rohe

We used to think that if we knew one, we knew two, because one and one are two.
We are finding that we must learn a great deal more about 'one'.

Sir Arthur Eddington

We need more understanding of human
nature, because the only real danger
that exists is man himself...
We know nothing of man, far too little.
His psyche should be studied because we
are the origin of all coming evil.

Carl Jung

Man with all his noble qualities, with sympathy that feels for the most debased, with benevolence which extends not only to other men but to the humblest living creature, with his god-like intellect which has penetrated into the movements and constitution of the solar system - with all these exalted powers - still bears in his bodily frame the indelible stamp of his lowly origin.

Charles Darwin

Illness is the doctor to whom we pay most heed: to kindness, to knowledge we make promises only; pain we obey.

Marcel Proust

He that will not apply new remedies must expect new evils;

for time is the greatest innovator.

Francis Bacon

This strange disease of modern life with its brisk

hurry and divided aims.

Matthew Arnold

History is the endless repetition of the wrong way of living,
and it'll start again tomorrow, if it's moved from here today.

Laurence Durrell

The eternal triangle.

Saying

It would take only one generation of forgetfulness to put us

back intellectually several thousand years.

Dean Tollefson

Do not go gentle into that good night.

Rage, rage against the dying of the light.

Dylan Thomas

See the world as your self.
Have faith in the way things are.
Love the world as your self;
then you can care for all things.

Lao Tzu

The world is sacred

It can't be improved.

If you tamper with it, you'll ruin it.

If you treat it like an object, you'll lose it.

Lao Tzu

We see then how far the monuments of wit and learning are
more durable than the monuments of power, or of the hands.
For have not the verses of Homer continued twenty-five
hundred years or more, without the loss of a syllable
or letter, during which time infinite palaces,
temples, castles, cities have been
decayed or demolished?

Francis Bacon

In nature there are neither rewards nor punishments;
there are only consequences.

Robert G. Ingersoll

He had a triangular face, the details of which were vague though the outline was clear, like a negative that had been left too long in the sun.

Ada Leverson

There is nothing permanent except change.

Heracleitus

There is no wealth but life.

John Ruskin

Truth sits upon the lips
of dying men.
Matthew Arnold

Brute force without wisdom falls by its own weight.

Horace

I always say that beauty is only sin deep.

Saki (H. H. Munro)

Power never takes a step back - only in the face of more power.

Malcolm X

The way up is the way down.

Heracleitus

He bears the seed of ruin in himself.

Matthew Arnold

We should weep for men at their birth,

not their death.

Charles, Baron de Montesquieu

Death is not the greatest loss in life. The greatest loss in life is what dies inside us while we live.

Norman Cousins

I believe in Heaven and Hell - on Earth.

Abraham L. Feinberg

The continuous labour of your life is to build the house of death.

Michel De Montaigne

Man has lost the capacity to foresee and to forestall.

He will end by destroying the earth.

Albert Schweitzer

We must reform if we would conserve.

Franklin Delano Roosevelt

The ink of the scholar is more sacred than the blood of the martyr.

Mohammed

I have often thought upon death, and I find it the least of all evils.

Francis Bacon

But I grow old always learning many things.

Solon

Nature's laws affirm instead of prohibit.
If you violate her laws you are your own
prosecuting attorney, judge, jury,
and hangman.

Luther Burbank

Men have an extraordinarily erroneous opinion of their position in nature;
and the error is ineradicable.

W. Somerset Maugham

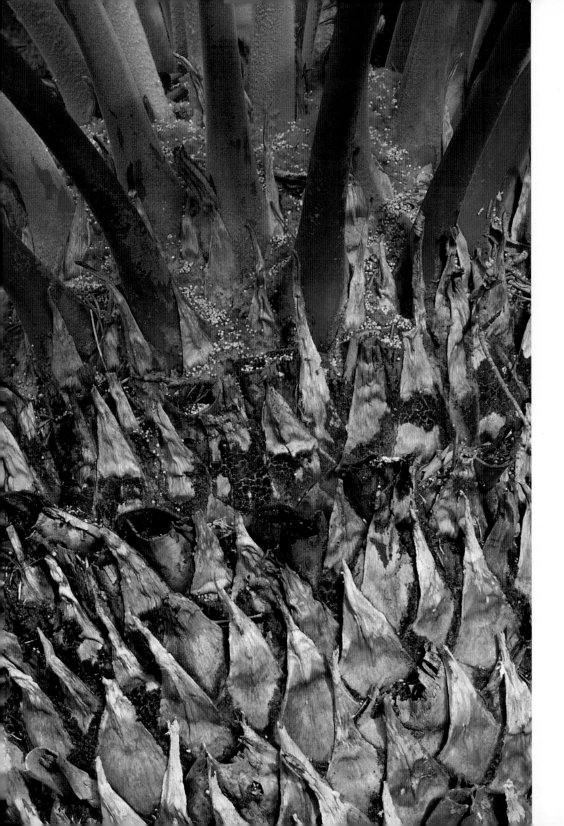

A man-cub is a man-cub, and he must learn

the Law of the Jungle.

Rudyard Kipling

The Law of the Jungle - which is by far

the oldest law in the world.

Rudyard Kipling

Laws are like cobwebs, for any trifling or powerless thing falls into them, they hold it fast; but if a thing of any size falls into them, it breaks the mesh and escapes.

Anacharsis

We have been God-like in our planned breeding of our
domesticated plants and animals, but we have been rabbit-like
in our unplanned breeding of ourselves.

Arnold Toynbee

Scientific and humanist approaches are not competitive but supportive,

and both are ultimately necessary.

Robert C. Wood

The universe shows evidence of a designing or controlling power
that has... the tendency to think in the way
which, for want of a better word,
we describe as mathematical.

Sir James Jeans

Any interference with nature is damnable. Not only nature but also the people will suffer.

Anahario (wife of Grey Owl)

We won't have a society if we destroy the environment.

Margaret Mead

178

*Nature will not allow humanity to be deprived of
the vision of Reality for very long.*

Maharishi Mahesh Yogi

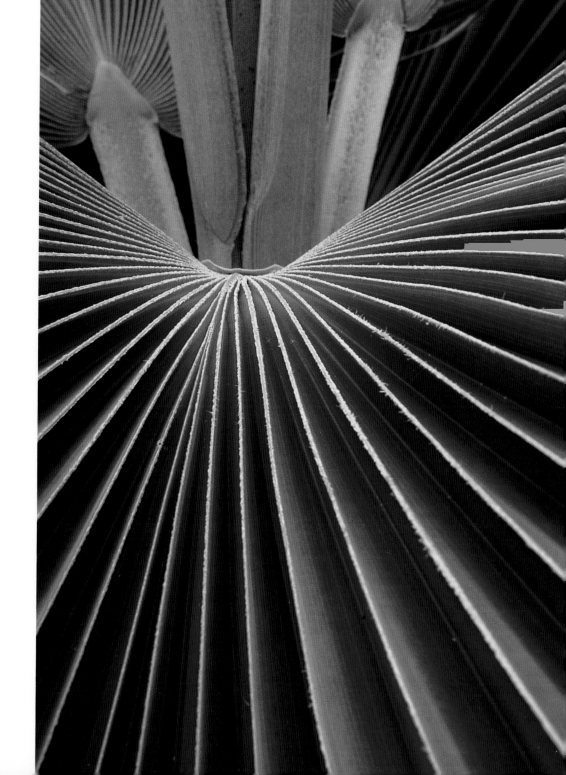

*The control man has secured over nature has far outrun
his control over himself.*

Ernest Jones

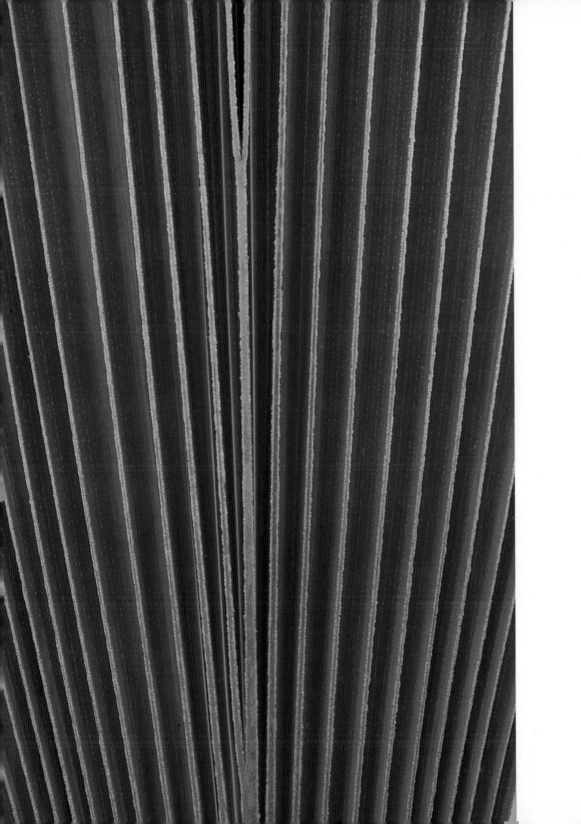

Let us permit nature to have her own way;
she understands her business better than we do.

Michel De Montaigne

Nature is proving that she can't be beaten - not by the likes of us.
She's taking the world away from the intellectuals
and giving it back to the apes.

Robert E. Sherwood

Never does nature say one thing and wisdom another.

Juvenal

Nature to be commanded, must be obeyed.

Francis Bacon

Everything that happens happens as it should,
and if you observe carefully,
you will find this to be so.

Marcus Aurelius Antoninus

Remember this, that there is a proper value and proportion
to be observed in the performance of every act.

Marcus Aurelius Antoninus

*Remember that to change your mind and follow him who sets you right
is to be none the less free than you were before.*

Marcus Aurelius Antoninus

In formal logic, a contradiction is the signal of defeat;

but in the evolution of real knowledge

it marks the first step in progress

towards victory.

Alfred North Whitehead

Character is destiny.

Heracleitus

Destiny is not a matter of chance, it is a matter of choice;

it is not a thing to be waited for:

it is a thing to be achieved.

William Jennings Bryan

Today the pressure is on, but we have a choice.
Mankind can either lie down and give up, or
we can use all of our productive skills and
knowledge to work for a better future.

Earl Butz

We never stop investigating. We are never satisfied that we know enough to get by.
Every question we answer leads on to another question. This has become the
greatest survival trick of our species.

Desmond Morris

If error is corrected whenever it is recognized as
such, the path of error is the path of truth.

Hans Reichenbach

Error of opinion may be tolerated where reason is
left free to combat it.

Thomas Jefferson

If we can really understand the problem, the answer will come out of it,
because the answer is not separate from the problem.

Krishnamurti

The ultimate value of life depends upon awareness, and the power of
contemplation rather than on mere survival.

Aristotle

What is honoured in a country will be cultivated there.

Plato

The great law of culture: let each become all that he [she] was created capable of being.

Thomas Carlyle

The future influences the present just as much as the past.

Freidrich Nietzsche

The farther back you can look, the farther forward you are likely to see.

Winston Churchill

Who controls the past controls the future.
Who controls the present controls the past.

George Orwell

The formula for Utopia on earth remains the same:

to make a necessity of virtue.

Clifton Fadiman

Eternal vigilance is the price of liberty.

Wendell Phillips

Liberty, too, must be limited

in order to be possessed.

Edmund Burke